I'm Trying to Be Like
JESUS

Text © 2010 Cynthia L. Dobson
Illustrations © 2010 Altus Fine Art, LLC

All rights reserved. No part of this book may be reproduced in any form or by any means without permission in writing from the publisher, Deseret Book Company, P. O. Box 30178, Salt Lake City, Utah 84130. This work is not an official publication of The Church of Jesus Christ of Latter-day Saints. The views expressed herein are the responsibility of the author and do not necessarily represent the position of the Church or of Deseret Book Company.

DESERET BOOK is a registered trademark of Deseret Book Company.

Visit us at DeseretBook.com

Library of Congress Cataloging-in-Publication Data
Dobson, Cynthia Lund.
  I'm trying to be like Jesus / Cynthia Lund Dobson ; illustrated by Simon Dewey.
    p. cm.
  ISBN 978-1-60641-846-8 (hardbound : alk. paper)
  1. Jesus Christ—Example—Juvenile literature. 2. Mormon children—Religious life—Juvenile literature. I. Dewey, Simon. II. Title.
  BX8643.C56D63 2010
   232.9'04—dc22   2010022505

Printed in the United States of America   10/2010
Inland Graphics, Menomonee Falls, WI

10 9 8 7 6 5 4 3 2 1

I'm Trying to Be Like JESUS

Cynthia L. Dobson

Illustrations by Simon Dewey

Salt Lake City, Utah

For I have given you an example,
that ye should do as I have done to you.

John 13:15

Jesus came to Earth to be an example.

I'm trying to be like Jesus
and follow His example.

Jesus prayed.

I can pray.

Jesus read the scriptures.

I can read the scriptures.

Jesus was baptized.

I can be baptized.

Jesus was loving.

I can be loving to my family and friends.

Jesus was kind to people who were different from him.

I can be kind to people who are different from me.

Jesus was forgiving.

I can be forgiving.

Jesus taught about tithing.

I can pay my tithing.

Jesus gave us the sacrament.

I can take the sacrament
and think about Jesus.

Jesus went to the temple.

I can prepare to go to the temple.

I know if I follow the example of Jesus,
I can be happy and I can return
and live with Him again.